# CREATING YOUR SOUL MAP

*A guide to finding calmness, harmony and wisdom*

## By Alison Wem

*Love*

*Alison Wem*

First published in 2018 by Alison Wem

ISBN 978-1-9997014-1-3

Alison Wem
Visit my website at www.yoursoulfamily.com

Edited by Steven Hiatt

Cover design by Jessica Bell

Names have been changed to protect the identity and privacy of those involved.

# Contents

Preface                                                                                                   v

Chapter 1: Introduction                                                                    1

Chapter 2: Seven Steps for Creating Your Soul Map              7

Chapter 3: Choosing a Soul Map Template                             11

    Daffodil-Inspired Template                                              12

    Celtic Cross-Inspired Template                                       14

    Tibetan Buddhism-Inspired Template                         16

    Hexagram-Inspired Template                                          18

    Interlocking Circles: Islam-Inspired Template            20

    Balance, Symmetry and Infinity–Inspired Template   21

    Spiral-Inspired Template                                                23

Foundation Soul Map Template                                    25

Hints and Tips                                                  26

Chapter 4: Designing Your Soul Map                              29

Chapter 5: Colouring Your Soul Map                              31

Chapter 6: Gaining More Meaning from the Colours in Your Soul Map   33

Chakras                                                         34

Chapter 7: Reflecting on Your Soul Map                          37

Chapter 8: Benefits of Creating and Continuing to Use Your Soul Map   39

After I Have Built My Soul Map, What Next?                      43

Next in the Your Soul Family Series                             46

Appendix: Your Soul Family Templates                            47

# Preface

I came to Your Soul Family some years ago. In the space of three years all of my near family passed away except for my brother, who was a six-hour journey away. The hardest passing was when I was unexpectedly widowed. My son was then fifteen years old and my daughter had just had her eleventh birthday party. I really did not know how I was going to cope with raising two children alone, running a home and holding down a demanding full-time job. I was on the go from 6 a.m. to 11 p.m. and then not sleeping well. I knew that this pace was not sustainable, but I did not know how to change my life. I felt so alone and unloved.

Many readers will have had similar experiences of bereavement, or extreme stress that can arise from any number of situations. Many of them involve loss of someone or something you value – a child, partner, job, business, home.  Each of us needs to find a way of handling our loss or stress.

It was in the early hours of a morning when sleep eluded me that I stumbled on my inner consciousness and found a space of calmness. It was there that I let out all of my hurt and loneliness – but to my great surprise it was there that I found strength, love and guidance. At last I had met my 'inner you'. Some people call this 'inner you' your sub-conscious, higher self or soul, depending on their life view. I like 'inner you' as it feels more familiar, someone close to you and not ethereal.

Meeting my 'inner you' was a real turning point for me. My key question was

### What should I do next in my life?

I knew I could not continue my life as it was, but I did not know how to change it for the better. Over time, my 'inner you' guided me in making small changes that made my life more manageable.

One of the life lessons I needed to learn was to be able to receive. I had always been a capable person, usually the one organising others and giving of myself. It took the dramatic event of becoming a widow to make me realise that I needed to be more balanced and to receive as well as to give. It was a hard life lesson for me, and it did not come to me easily. In the early months of widowhood, I survived through the kindness of friends, through their practical gifts of collecting a child from school, fixing things in the home when they went wrong, providing a meal when I was exhausted and calling me so I did not feel so alone.

After I first stumbled on my place of calmness, it took me some time to learn to communicate with my 'inner you'. It required trial and error plus repeating things many times over a number of weeks to see if I received the same answers. It took me some time to get to know my 'inner you' and to learn to trust the messages I received.

To make your journey easier, the Your Soul Family series of books captures the processes of getting to know your 'inner you', so you too can have a friend to aid you as you encounter challenges on your journey of life. In this process you will create and colour a geometric picture of you and your life which I have called a 'Soul Map', as a visual aid to understanding yourself better. No artistic skills are required.

Through a number of exercises, you will get to know your 'inner you' and learn to ask simple questions to receive your own wisdom. This guide with its simple-to-follow steps is the first in this series. I strongly believe that your 'inner you' will enrich your life and will guide you in enhancing your own personal development.

No matter where you are in life's journey, no-one is too old, too clever or too wise to learn new things. Your Soul Family is a new approach to personal development which bridges the scientific approaches of the 20th century and the mystical approaches of past ages to help us to cope with the bustle of living in the 21st century.

Give it a try with this short book, which provides easy-to-follow steps in creating your Soul Map to meet your 'inner you'.

Best wishes,
*Alison Wem*

# Chapter 1:
# Introduction

*Creating Your Soul Map* is about getting back in touch with your subconscious mind, higher self or soul, depending on your personal beliefs. To encompass all of these beliefs, I have chosen to call it your 'inner you'.

*Creating Your Soul Map* enables you to connect with your 'inner you' and find a place of calmness where you can receive insights into your life. This connection often leads to creating more harmony in your life and facilitates you re-discovering your personal wisdom. You are guided through some clear steps to create a map that leads you back from your conscious mind to your 'inner you'. I have chosen to call this picture your Soul Map.

> ℘℧
>
> Soul Maps are a visual
> representation of you
> and your life.
>
> ℘℧

Each one is a geometric picture; an example of one is at the start of this chapter. The outer circle of the Soul Map represents the circle of life. You are the circle in the middle. The other circles represent people who are important in your life. They can be from your blood family, in-laws, adopted family, friends and colleagues. You are all interacting with one another in what I call your Soul Family.

The lines between members of your family represent either a life lesson you are helping each other with or a special relationship. Examples of life lessons might be learning to listen, to be patient, or to define and hold your boundaries. When the life lesson is not clear to you, often it is the presence of a special relationship that alerts you to a lesson being learnt. Examples might include a special relationship between a grandfather and a grandson where the thing in common is the same sense of humour or a love of music. Often that certain something which makes a relationship special is quite small and perhaps hard to identify but is nevertheless very important.

Creating your own Soul Map aids connection between your conscious you and your subconscious you. That is why I call this picture a Soul Map – it charts the route back from your conscious you to your 'inner you'. Meditating or reflecting on your Soul Map continues to strengthen communication with your 'inner you'. Once you are in contact with your 'inner you', you can ask a question about your life and receive a meaningful answer. It might not always be the answer you want, but it will be the right message for you based on where you are in your life at that time.

Soul Maps are secular in nature but use geometric shapes that are found across many cultures, religions and nations. You can find them in many places, and in many contexts. Below are some examples of such geometric designs:

Manhole covers, London.

Islamic patterns: Alcazar, Seville, showing patterns that are both finite and infinite.

Mandala: a circular figure representing the
universe in Hindu and Buddhist symbolism.

Over the centuries the human psyche has been attracted to these patterns, many of which are used by people in reflection or meditation. They are patterns which please the human mind.

*Geometry is a universal language* that enables you to unlock knowledge contained in your subconscious about the true nature of yourself. Your subconscious mind can have a powerful awareness of you. Often there are things about yourself that you know in a vague way, but that are not fully apparent to your conscious self – for example, what caused a phobia you experience, such as claustrophobia. Or you have a real dislike of someone but you do not know why. As you go through the process of creating your Soul Map you will gain more insight into yourself, making these things more explicit to your conscious you.

*To help you in this creation process,* we provide a selection of templates you can choose from as the basis of your Soul Map. Once you have chosen your template, you will need to consider who is important in your life and where you would place them in your Soul Map. Then you should think about the relationships between these people and how or whether they are helping each other with life lessons such as patience or listening.

> ℘ ℃
>
> As you colour, the 'inner you' will connect with your picture and bring relaxation and calmness.
>
> ℘ ℃

5

When you have the general layout of your Soul Map and placed individuals in your family circle, the next stage is to colour your Soul Map. No artistic skills are required as the picture is made of geometric shapes. Adding colour brings energy and vitality into your picture. As you colour, the 'inner you' will connect with your picture and bring relaxation and calmness. In that calm space within you, you will find a wisdom you did not know you possessed.

Your 'inner you' is a loving friend, with you always and
trying to guide you on your journey through life.

In making the decisions on the shape and colour of your Soul Map, the best advice I can give you is to do what feels right. If it feels good to you, it is the right decision. Of course, as you get to know yourself more, you may change your mind on some things and want to re-do your Soul Map. That is all right and as it should be. Life is a voyage of discovery.

6

# Chapter 2: Seven Steps for Creating Your Soul Map

Here is a quick summary of the steps you need to take to create your Soul Map. You have already taken the biggest step, which is to find out about your 'inner you'. You are now just seven simple steps from creating your own Soul Map, the route back to your 'inner you'.

> ෨ ෬
>
> You have already taken the biggest step – deciding to find out about your 'inner you'.
>
> ෨ ෬

1. Find a quiet space where you will not be disturbed.

2. Choose a template from the selection provided in this book. Choose the one that pleases you the most. You can use your chosen template in the Appendix

of this book, or you can go to 'Free Your Soul Family templates' at www. yoursoulfamily.com and download and print it. It will be larger than the pictures in this book and is the starting point for creating your own Soul Map.

3.  You are the circle in the middle. The other circles are people who are important in your life and may be helping you with the life lessons you want to learn. Think about whom they may be and where you would place them in the circle. Do you have an inner circle of supporters? If so, place these individuals in the circles nearest to you.

4.  Think about the colour that would represent you the best. Colour your circle with water colours, chalk, felt pens or acrylic paint. All are easy to obtain in the high street. You want the colour to be rich and vibrant, so be careful not to use too much water with the paints.

5.  Do the same for each of your family members.

6.  Before you start to colour your Soul Map, ask yourself: "What is the message that I need to hear at this moment in my life?"

    Relax and enjoy colouring this picture of you for you. Feel the calmness start to come in.

7.  Your message will arrive in the next few days. It may come in some unexpected ways – as a knowing, a dream, a phrase on the radio echoing a thought or a billboard picture or words jumping out at you. Be alert so you are able to receive your message when and how it chooses to arrive.

If after a while you are unsure whether you have received your message correctly, repeat the question again while you are reflecting on your Soul Map. Wait to see what answer you get. If the message is the same as the original one, it is highly likely you received it correctly. This is not a process to rush. Take your time to receive your message.

# Chapter 3: Choosing a Soul Map Template

We have seven templates to choose from. Choose a template that you feel reflects the shape and dynamics of your family. If a template is not quite right for you, do not be afraid to change it. It is important that the template becomes your own. If none of the templates pleases you, you can build the centre of your picture yourself. There is an eighth template, a foundation one, which you can use if you wish to take this route. It is made up of the outer circle, your circle of family members and yourself to help you to get going. You then need to focus on the design of the central area.

Each template represents shapes from different cultural and religious backgrounds. You can look at them and see which one seems most suitable as the basis of the first colouring of your Soul Map. Do not be surprised if you are attracted to a template that does not reflect your own cultural or religious background. There will be a reason for your choice which will probably become apparent to you later on.

**It is really important that you choose a template that appeals to you and not one you feel you should choose simply because of your background or religion.**

See which one resonates with you. Don't make a selection until you have gone through all of them. Be confident you have made the right choice for where you and your Soul Family are at this moment in time. As you become familiar with the process, you might decide to create another Soul Map with a different template as you and your family have changed.

> ❧ ❧
>
> Choose a template that reflects the shape and dynamics of your family.
>
> ❧ ❧

## Daffodil-Inspired Template

Sometimes nature can help us to decide what would be an appropriate shape for the inner portion of our Soul Map. The daffodil blooms in the spring and represents new beginnings. This Soul Map contains the geometric shapes found in a daffodil.

A daffodil.

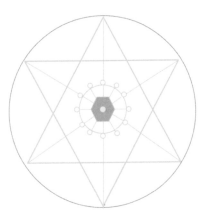

The structure of the daffodil forms the
foundation of the daffodil template.

© 2015 Alison Wern

Daffodil-inspired template.

*This family has six key family members and a strong inner circle to support you. The two equilateral triangles that join the six key family members represent achieving or practising balance within the family.*

## Celtic Cross-Inspired Template

This template has two powerful symbols, the circle and the cross. The outer circle of life is re-emphasised by the inner circles and symbolises the endless path of knowledge. The cross represents the physical world and resides over these circles. The arms of the cross signify the North, South, East and West.

Replica Celtic broach.

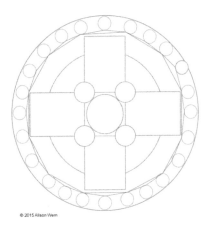

© 2015 Alison Wern

Celtic Cross–inspired template.

*This family feels strong and is very grounded and practical. You have a select number of supporters in your inner circle, but they are significant in your life. You know and understand each other well.*

## Tibetan Buddhism-Inspired Template

Mandalas are an ancient Eastern art form. Traditional mandalas, often created by Buddhist monks, can be deeply elaborate representations of nirvana. The word 'mandala' is a Sanskrit word meaning 'circle' or 'enclosure'. It was first recorded in the ancient Hindu scripture Rig Veda and is an integral part of the sacred art of Hinduism, Buddhism and Jainism, the three great traditions that originated in India. However, it is with the Buddhist tradition, in particular Tibetan Buddhism, that mandalas are most commonly associated.

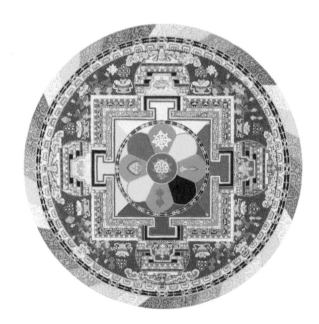

Example of a Tibetan mandala.

Although mandalas are particularly associated with the East, they have in fact been an important feature of Western traditions as well.  One of the most ancient and powerful symbols is the cross. In Christianity one of the best-known examples is the Celtic Cross encompassed by a circle. The centre of the cross is also in the centre of the circle. The four arms of the cross represent the four physical dimensions – North, South, East and West and provide the link between the circle of the heavens and the Earth below. It is thought that the Celtic cross pre-dates Christianity and was adopted by early Christianity before Roman Christianity became more dominant and introduced the cross of Christ. The halo that surrounds the head of Christ and the saints in Christian art is also an echo of the mandala circle.

This template is inspired by the Tibetan mandala, which has a square within the circle to represent the knowledge that the teacher wants to give to the pupil.

The multiple lines represent the life lessons and skills available within the family. This brings the opportunity for wisdom to be available to you. You are represented by the figure in the centre and supported by two key family members. The multiple connections you have to your outer circle are a mix of passed family members, your generation and the next. This arrangement serves to remind you of the transient nature of life.

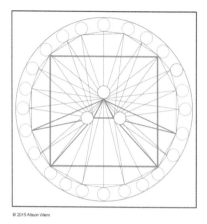

© 2015 Alison Wern

Tibetan Buddhism–inspired template.

*This family has learnt many life lessons and has wisdom available to them. However, they do not always remember their lessons and use the skills available to them. They are reaching out to each other to improve their overall learning. You are a central figure in this process and the figure in the centre of this Soul Map represents you.*

## Hexagram-Inspired Template

A pair of overlaid equilateral triangles creates a six-pointed star with a hexagon in the middle. It is known as the Star of David in Judaism and is a Hindu mandala symbol called 'Sadkona Yantra'. It is a widely used symbol and is also found in Christianity, The Latter-Day Saints (Mormons), Islam, Occult and Theosophy.

Example of a Sadkona Yantra.

The two interlocking triangles represent balance. It is also 'the Heart Chakra' symbol, which has twelve lotus petals around it. Originating from Hinduism and Tantric Buddhism, a chakra is an energy centre in our bodies through which energy flows. The Heart Chakra is either green or pink and is associated with emotions, unconditional love and compassion.

© 2015 Alison Wem

Hexagram–inspired template.

19

*This family is trying to or has achieved some balance and is practising unconditional love. Achieving inner peace is a core value of this family. The small triangles within the hexagram represent accumulated human experiences this family has attained. Being in their Soul Map serves to remind them of the experiences through which they have learnt or are learning their life lessons to acquire greater insight and wisdom. They are integral to achieving inner peace and harmony.*

## Interlocking Circles: Islam-Inspired Template

The shape of a mosque is often based on five domes arranged around a double axis. These can be adorned with more domes depending on the size and grandeur of the mosque. However, the core shape often remains the same. A circle in 3D is a sphere, so the dome reflects the transition between Earth and the Heavens.

Sultan Ahmed (Blue) Mosque, Istanbul.

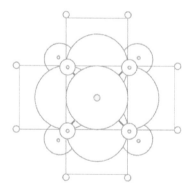

Ahmed Sultan (Blue) Mosque floor plan.

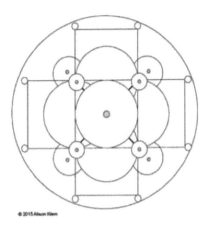

© 2015 Alison Warm

Interlocking circles: Islam-inspired template.

*This family has many members clustered at the heart of the family. You are supported by four key family members, who in turn are supported by a further three. Supportive emotionally of one another, this family offers practical support when facing out into the physical world. This practical strength comes from the underlying equilateral cross, which is the foundation of this template.*

## Balance, Symmetry and Infinity–Inspired Template

Like the Sri Yantra diagram in the Hindu faith, this template draws the eye to the centre as if through a tunnel, reflecting Man's journey through the cosmos and taking us back to the moment of creation. The centre represents the beginning: the universe, our family, ourselves. The triangles represent physical existences which make up our world. For each family member in the rim there are multiple triangles. They have had many life experiences and opportunities to learn. The circle symbolises that this has been happening for a long time. Our world expressed in geometric shapes and mathematical formulae helps us to understand it and to appreciate the balance and symmetry within it. The universe and the cosmos stretch out into infinity, as represented at the central point of this template.

The Sri Yantra is a form of mystical diagram, known as a yantra and found in the Shri Vidva school of Hindu tantra. It is made up of nine interlocking triangles which represent the cosmos.

Example of a Sri Yantra.

*This family has acquired much wisdom from life experiences. The family members are joined in a circle and work with all in their family rather than in key hubs. They are comfortable sharing within their family group. This template shows that you have an inner circle of supporters which have been with you for as long as you can remember.*

© 2015 Alison Wern

Balance, symmetry and infinity-inspired template.

## Spiral-Inspired Template

Spirals are found all around us in nature and have had a significance place in the human psyche since Stone Age man.

Nature's spirals.

Avebury stone circle, reflecting ancient man's interest in spirals.

Replica Celtic jewellery.

The interlocking triple spiral on the next page represents the meeting of sky, earth and water, the intertwining of the past, present and future, and the progress of learning and acquiring knowledge. Balance and movement co-exist, coming together in the calmness of the centre.

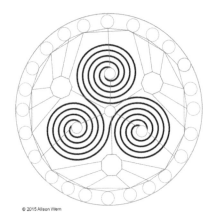

© 2015 Alison Wern

Spirals–inspired template.

*This family is in the process of change. The triple spiral represents transformation. The family is learning from life events experienced by family members and are adapting their behaviour and learning new skills. You have three key supporters in your inner circle, and each in turn is the lead person in key clusters within the family. You have a second circle of supporters at the centre of each spiral. These six people help the family with maintaining its balance as they transform. You are central to holding the whole together and the point from which the calmness radiates outwards.*

## Foundation Soul Map Template

If you choose to design your own central area to your Soul Map, we provide a foundation template to help you start. You may decide to use a variation on one of the templates provided or develop a totally different design. However, it is

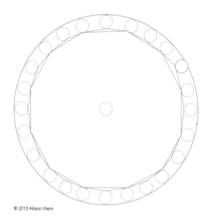

© 2015 Alison Wern

Foundation template.

worth remembering that your 'inner you' appreciates balance and symmetry. Your design is likely to please you more if it is organised and balanced rather than chaotic.

## Hints and Tips

In choosing your template to represent your family you can either be analytical or just feel what is right for you. How your family operates can guide you in your choice. In being analytical you can look at your family using the following pointers. Think about your family and decide:

- Does my family tend to have multiple clusters, a few key people, or many interactions?

- Do I have an inner circle of helpers? Are they a select few or a larger group?

- Are there many one-to-one relationships?

- Does my family feel in the midst of change, or is it mature with significant wisdom?

Or you can use your intuition, that feeling inside sometimes called your 'gut instinct', to ask your 'inner you' which feels the right template and choose it.

Both methods work well, and a blend of both is even better. The key thing is not to agonise but to choose. Have confidence that it will be the right choice for you.

# Chapter 4:
# Designing Your Soul Map

Some people like to take their template and jump straight in with colouring. Others like to consider the template and **where the important people in their life should sit** within it before they start to colour. The choice of approach is yours. If you decide to take the time to consider the layout of your Soul Map, the questions you might want to ask yourself are:

- Who are the important people in my life?

- Where would I place an individual on my Soul Map?

- What are the relationships between individuals?

- Do they have an important relationship with me?

- Is a life lesson being learnt?

- Who is helping with that life lesson?

- Is there a natural grouping of individuals—for example, a grandfather and grandson, or cousins who always gather together at family functions? If so, place them together in your Soul Map.

**Often life lessons show themselves as repeated challenges.** For me, one of my life lessons was about defining and maintaining my personal boundaries. Before I realised this, I had a series of very challenging managers, each getting progressively worse. I really wondered what I had done to deserve them. When I realised that they were helping me to learn a life lesson, I approached the situation differently and managed it much better. My next two managers were wonderful, so I must have gone some way to learning my lesson.

Do not be surprised if you **keep moving people around your picture** as you answer these questions. You will find that your 'inner you' appreciates balance and symmetry. As you place people in your Soul Map, use that sense of appreciation and enjoyment to guide your design.

The human brain remembers things best in **groups of three.** You may find that placement of people in groups of three, either by a special relationship or by colour, pleases your 'inner you'. Do not be surprised if this principle appears in your Soul Map.

# Chapter 5: Colouring Your Soul Map

This is the stage I love the most, as it is very rewarding. The first thing you will need to decide is the **material you will use to colour your picture.** Water colours, chalk, felt pens or acrylic paint, all are readily available in the high street. However, personally I would always choose paint. It takes more skill to use paints, so using them engages your brain sufficiently to still the noisy chatter it loves so much. And when you stop the brain's chatter, you allow the calmness to come in. This feeling of calmness in our busy 21st-century lives is wonderful and such a healing tonic.

Having chosen your colouring medium, most people choose to colour the circles representing **their family members and themselves first.** Each circle represents a person in your life, so you will want to choose a colour that feels right

to represent this person. You may also
consider different effects such as a darker
shade at the middle and a lighter one at
the edges or one colour in the centre and
another at the edges. Paints in particular
are very versatile and offer many options.
You may have a group of blue people, but

> ℰℴ ℭℛ
>
> Stopping the brain's chatter
> allows the calmness to come in.
>
> ℰℴ ℭℛ

they could be a variety of shades. Now is the time to let your 'inner you' steer
your choices and do just what feels right and pleases you.

**Now stand back and look at your Soul Map** to see the overall affect. If you
are not happy with it, there is always the option to download another copy of your
chosen template and start again.

The next choice to make is the background colours. They represent the
emotions, energy and presence of your combined family members. These colours
may not be uniform. Think of them as a mist swirling around your family. Choose
what feels right to you and pleases you.

# Chapter 6: Gaining More Meaning from the Colours in Your Soul Map

Individual family members may talk to you through using the energy from one or more of their chakras. Understanding the emotions associated with the chakras and their colours can give you vital clues as to the nature of the communication. It is through your emotions that you speak to the universe and the universal energy, so it is worth understanding colours and our emotions.

ॐ ☙ ❧

*Through your emotions you
speak to the universe.*

ॐ ☙ ❧

Below is a brief outline of the key chakras, where they are in the body, their colour and the emotions associated with them. To aid anyone who may be colour-blind, I have also added the symbols for each chakra so you can follow the meaning by shape rather than colour.

## CHAKRAS

Originating in Hinduism and adopted by Tantric Buddhism, chakras are energy centres in our bodies through which energy flows. There are seven key ones, which align with our spine up through our bodies. Each has a specific colour and shape and is associated with a specific organ and with specific emotions.

**Root Chakra.** Found at the base of our spine in the tailbone area. Red in colour, it is our foundation and addresses survival issues such as food, money and personal security.

**Sacral Chakra.** Found in the lower abdomen about two inches below the navel. Orange in colour, it's associated with abundance, well-being, pleasure and sexuality.

**Solar Plexus Chakra.** Found in the upper abdomen in the stomach area. Yellow in colour, it relates to our ability to be confident and in control of our lives. It gives us our self-worth, self-confidence and self-esteem.

**Heart Chakra.** Found in the centre of the chest just above our heart. Green in colour, it is all about our ability to love, to give and to receive love. It gives us our love, joy and inner peace.

**Throat Chakra.** Found in the throat. Blue in colour, this is the energy of communication, how we express our feelings and the truth.

**Third Eye Chakra.** Found in the forehead between the eyes. Indigo in colour, it is linked to our intuition, imagination, wisdom, ability to think and make decisions.

**Crown Chakra.** Found at the very top of the head. Mauve in colour, it is here we find our connection to spirituality, pure bliss.

Chakra energy centers.                                    Chakra symbols.

# Chapter 7:
# Reflecting on Your
# Soul Map

After you have created your Soul Map, using it for reflection or in meditation will enhance the quality and depth of your experience.

**Flicker your eyes across your Soul Map and feel your calmness return.**

As you look at your Soul Map, thank your 'inner you' for helping you to create it. Look at yourself in the middle, and then move your eyes outwards to your inner circle of supporters and then your family members. Be thankful that they are in your life helping you with your life lessons. Remember the insight you received as you created your Soul Map and the feelings you experienced when you coloured it. Remember the relaxation and calmness, and savour it again.

In that calm space, you will be able to ask key questions about your life to receive fresh insight. These may not arrive instantly but over the coming days and weeks you will receive an answer if you are alert. The answer may arrive as a knowing, or in a dream or as something that jumps out at you—perhaps in the words of a song on the radio or the message on a billboard. Be assured it will arrive; you just need to learn to relax and be receptive to it. Keep the question simple to aid clarity and ask only one question at a time.

Soul Maps are also useful in moments of stress. I used to keep my Soul Map on my desk at work when I was in a stressful corporate job. Whenever everything was chaotic I used to flicker my eyes across my Soul Map and feel my calmness return, as though my 'inner you' had given me a big hug. I was then able to cope with my chaotic world more readily.

Having a Soul Map at home in the kitchen is also a popular location. Families often congregate in the kitchen and important conversations in your life often happen there. Your kitchen Soul Map can bring you calmness in handling your life at home.

It is quite all right to paint several Soul Maps so you can have one in several locations. It is not unusual to find that you have emphasised different colours in your Soul Maps if your needs are different in each location.

# Chapter 8:
## Benefits of Creating and Continuing to Use Your Soul Map

There are great benefits to be gained from creating your own Soul Map. It brings pleasure and a greater understanding of your life and your family as you create it. I have found that this greater understanding has **brought more harmony into my family.** As you understand each individual's needs better, your behaviour towards them is more appropriate. As you colour your Soul Map, relaxation and calmness arrive, and in that calm space you connect with your 'inner you'.

> ✇ ❧
>
> Greater understanding brings more harmony into your family.
>
> ✇ ❧

To summarise the benefits of Creating Your Soul Map, you will have:

- commenced looking at your **life to date** and identified where **repeated challenges** are being presented to you. These represent **life lessons for you to learn** or practise.

- **started to understand** the reasons for the challenges. This often results in you **approaching each challenge in a more positive frame of mind.** Challenges are an opportunity to learn rather than you being a victim of misfortune.

- **gained insight into your life and lessons,** which provides you with the **opportunity for enhanced self-development.**

- learned a **mechanism for achieving calmness** and being able to hear the **voice of your 'inner you'.**

- taken the opportunity to use your Soul Map in **meditation to enhance your relaxation and connection** to your 'inner you'. When you meditate with your Soul Map you will remember your family's dynamics, your relationships and the lessons you are learning. The calmness you experienced while colouring your Soul Map starts to return. In that calm space, you can have a dialogue with your 'inner you' and explore further the dynamics of your life and your family. Great insight and wisdom can be accessed.

- arranged your Soul Map on your desk or in your kitchen or any other place where you are busy and can glance at it during moments of stress. You will start to feel the **calmness return to you.**

Soul Families are dynamic, as life events affect and change how you and your family feel. Expect over time that you will feel the urge to create a new Soul Map. This often happens when there are changes in your life.

An example, one of my earliest students, Andrea, has painted the following Soul Maps. They represent her life journey to date.

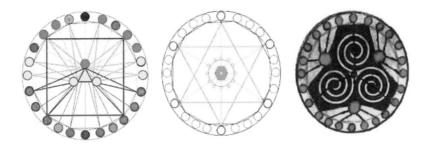

Andrea's Soul Maps.

The first one Andrea created was while she was in fact-gather mode and learning about herself and her Soul Family. There are many different people, colours, lessons and special relationships. This was a period of learning, and Andrea is a strong, central figure in her Soul Map. This Soul Map became one of our templates.

The second Soul Map reflects a period of change in Andrea's life: one chapter of her life was finishing and another one starting. Daffodils come in the spring, and this template represents new beginnings.

Andrea's last Soul Map represents transformation and is from a period in Andrea's life when she was in transformation at home and at work. Green is a colour for personal growth and unconditional love, joy and inner peace. Yellow is for confidence and self-esteem. I loved this Soul Map so much that Andrea agreed to let me use it as my logo. It has amazed me how many people respond to the signs for transformation in this Soul Map.

Creating a series of Soul Maps over time represents your life journey. For me, creating your own Soul Map brings insight into one's life and therefore the opportunity to transform. Used in reflection or meditation, your calmness is enhanced and the connection to your 'inner you' and your personal wisdom is amplified. The gift of creating and using your own Soul Map is just perfect for you.

**Remember, learning continues for your whole life. You are never too old to learn something new!**

> ℰℬ
>
> Creating a series of
> Soul Maps over time represents
> your life journey.
>
> ℰℬ

## After I Have Built My Soul Map, What Next?

Creating your Soul Map re-awakens the communications between your conscious mind and your 'inner you'. Your 'inner you' will be keen to send you insight so you have the opportunity to access your personal wisdom. To maximise the benefit from this connection, I would encourage you to:

1.  **Keep a Thought Diary.** You often receive insight as you wake up, in the shower and going to sleep. If you do not note down your thoughts you will know that you have had an insight but not be able to remember what it was! This can be very frustrating. At times of high activity, such as after creating a new Soul Map, I keep a post-it note pad by my bed and in the bathroom. As insight comes I make a quick note and later stick it in my Thought Diary. It gives me great pleasure to re-read them and to achieve a greater understanding of myself and my family.

2.  **Review your picture and continue to revise it.**

3.  **Paint another picture** to include your revisions.

4.  **Join the Your Soul Family community.** The home of our international community is at www.yoursoulfamily.com with articles on mindfulness at home and at work, comments and feedback, downloads of the templates, and Early Bird alerts of new publications.

5.  For those of you in the UK, consider:

    - **attending a workshop in London,** where we do a number of exercises to tease out what you know about yourself and your family to enrich the meaning in your Soul Map.

    - **hosting a Your Soul Family workshop for your friends** – with four paying guests, you go free. I am prepared to travel out of London.

    - attending **my regular evening course in London,** where you will learn to do your own design for the inner circle of your Soul Map

    Check the Your Soul Family Programme for the latest information on these options.

6.  For those of you outside the UK, there will soon be a book that leads you through many of the exercises from my workshops. I am also creating an online video course. Watch out for their releases or ask at www.yoursoulfamily.com for an Early Bird publication alert.

7.  There is a building 'Your Soul Family' community with people trying to bring these techniques into their lives both at work and at home. Your work person and home person are one. You should try to maintain your calmness and connection to your 'inner you' in both work and home arenas.

**Stay in touch with the Your Soul Family community, at www.yoursoulfamily.com**

Thank you for joining the Your Soul Family team. Did you enjoy *Creating Your Soul Map*? Here is what you can do next. If you have loved the book and have a moment to spare, I would really appreciate a short review.  Your help in spreading the word is gratefully received. The next in the Your Soul Family series will be available in the coming months. You can sign up to be notified of the next book as well as giveaways and pre-release specials at:

**www.yoursoulfamily.com sign-up form**

## Next in the Your Soul Family Series

*Finding Your Soul Family* – a guide to personal development. This book leads you through the steps to identify who is in your Soul Family, the life lessons you might be learning and who is assisting whom with them. It includes exercises from the Your Soul Family workshops and many examples of students' experiences on their voyage of self-discovery. *Finding Your Soul Family* will be published as an e-book and in print. For an Early Bird alert, visit **Finding Your Soul Family – publication alert at www.yoursoulfamily.com.**

Good luck with creating your Soul Map and your journey of self-discovery! I am sure it will bring you much pleasure. If you have any questions, please contact me through the Your Soul Family website at www.yoursoulfamily.com.

Best wishes,

Alison Wem

# Appendix
# Your Soul Family Templates

Daffodil-inspired template.

Celtic Cross-inspired template.

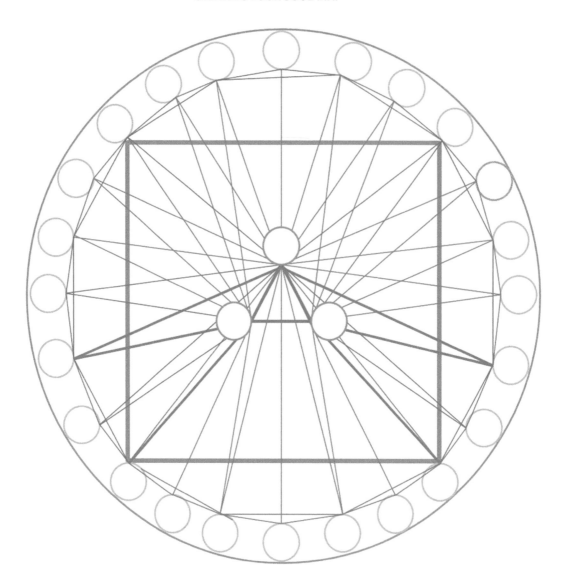

Tibetan Buddhism-inspired template.

Hexagram-inspired template.

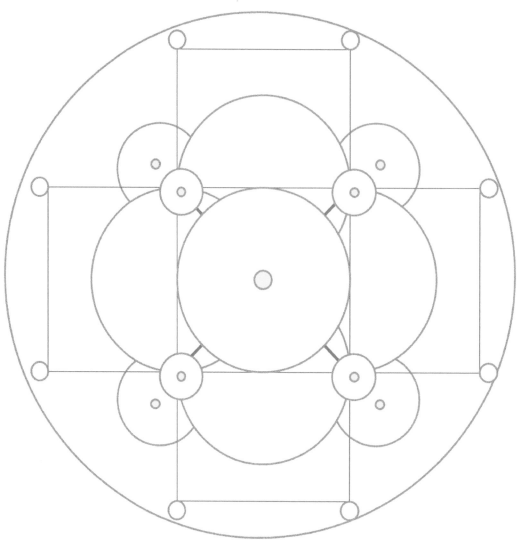

Interlocking circles: Islam-inspired template.

Balance, symmetry and infinity-inspired template.

Spiral-inspired template.

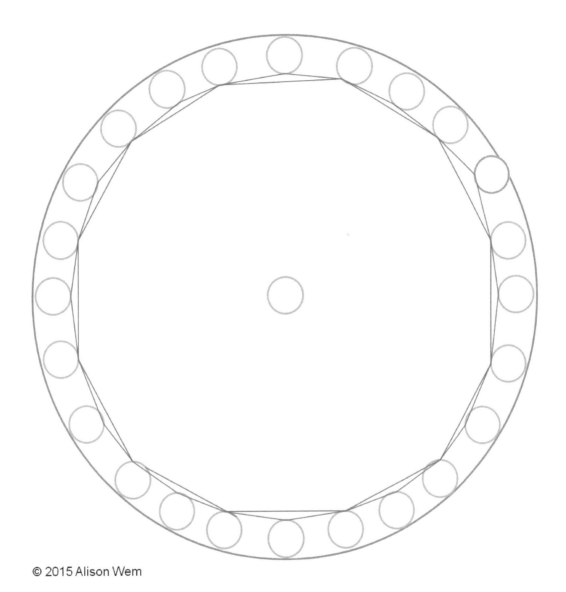

Foundation Soul Map template.

Lightning Source UK Ltd.
Milton Keynes UK
UKHW052327100119
335354UK00001B/1/P